critters by the sea

SEA LIONS ON THE SHORE

MELISSA RAÉ SHOFNER

PowerKiDS press.
New York

Published in 2018 by The Rosen Publishing Group, Inc.
29 East 21st Street, New York, NY 10010

First Edition

Editor: Melissa Raé Shofner
Book Design: Tanya Dellaccio

Photo Credits: Cover Andrea Nicola Luzio/EyeEm/Getty Images; pp. 3–24 (background image) Kemal Mardin/Shutterstock.com; p. 5 (walrus) Vladimir Melnik/Shutterstock.com; p. 5 (seal) worldswildlifewonders/Shutterstock.com; p. 5 (sea lion) Kanokratnok/Shutterstock.com; p. 6 chbaum/Shutterstock.com; pp. 7, 9 (top) Andrea Izzotti/Shutterstock.com; p. 9 (bottom) Yai/Shutterstock.com; p. 11 (seal) AEPhotographic/Shutterstock.com; p. 11 (sea lion) Shane W Thompson/Shutterstock.com; p. 13 Alex Mustard/Nature Picture Library/Getty Images; p. 14 Claudiovidri/Shutterstock.com; p. 15 Claude Huot/Shutterstock.com; p. 17 (top) Michael Melford/National Geographic/Getty Images; p. 17 (bottom) Bildagentur Zoonar GmbH/Shutterstock.com; p. 19 Rüdiger Katterwe/EyeEm/Getty Images; p. 21 Courtesy of Navy.mil; p. 22 Eric Isselee/Shutterstock.com.

Cataloging-in-Publication Data

Names: Shofner, Melissa Raé.
Title: Sea lions on the shore / Melissa Raé Shofner.
Description: New York : PowerKids Press, 2018. | Series: Critters by the sea | Includes index.
Identifiers: ISBN 9781538325896 (pbk.) | ISBN 9781538325193 (library bound) | ISBN 9781538325902 (6 pack)
Subjects: LCSH: Sea lions–Juvenile literature.
Classification: LCC QL737.P63 S56 2018 | DDC 599.79'75–dc23

Manufactured in the United States of America

CPSIA Compliance Information: Batch #BW18PK: For Further Information contact Rosen Publishing, New York, New York at 1-800-237-9932

CONTENTS

MEET THE PINNIPEDS

Sea lions aren't lions that live in the sea. You'd probably mistake a sea lion for a seal before you'd mistake one for a lion. So where does their name come from? Some people think sea lions are named for the lionlike mane many of the males have. Others say it's their lionlike roar.

Sea lions, true seals, and walruses belong to a group of animals called pinnipeds, which means "**flipper** footed." All pinnipeds have four paddlelike flippers that help them swim.

SEA CREATURE FEATURE

Sea lions are a type of seal, but they aren't "true" seals. Sea lions have earflaps, but true seals don't. Instead, true seals have ear holes.

Pinnipeds live in the water, but they aren't fish. They're mammals. Like all mammals, pinnipeds breathe air, are warm-blooded, have fur or hair, and make milk to feed their young.

SEA LIONS AROUND THE WORLD

Sea lions live around the world. They can be found in every ocean except the northern Atlantic. There are several **species** of sea lions. South American sea lions, Australian sea lions, and New Zealand sea lions live in the Southern **Hemisphere**.

Sea lions also live in the Northern Hemisphere. California sea lions make their homes along North America's Pacific coast, from Mexico to British Columbia, Canada. Some Steller's sea lions live on the California coast. However, most prefer to live in colder waters near the Bering Sea and Alaska.

STELLER'S SEA LION

SEA CREATURE FEATURE

Steller's sea lions are the largest species of sea lion. Males can weigh more than 1 ton (0.9 t)!

Sea lions like to spend time on rocky shorelines and sandy beaches. However, most of their time is spent swimming in the ocean.

FLIPPERS AND FUR

Sea lions have a long, pointed **snout** with **whiskers**. Their tube-shaped bodies are covered in short, thin hairs. Their coats come in many shades of brown but look black and shiny when wet.

Sea lions' large foreflippers, or front flippers, look like wings. Their hind, or back, flippers are flat with five long, **webbed** toes. Sea lions move their foreflippers up and down to swim quickly through the water. Their hind flippers are used to direct their movements while they swim.

SEA CREATURE FEATURE

Sea lions fold their hind flippers under their body when they're on land. This helps them walk!

Sea lions are very good swimmers. Their strong flippers help them swim quickly and easily.

CAN YOU SPOT THE DIFFERENCE

Sometimes people aren't sure if they're looking at a sea lion or a true seal. However, there are a few easy ways to tell the two animals apart. Start by looking at the animal's ears. Sea lions have small earflaps on the sides of their head. True seals have only tiny openings.

Sea lions and true seals also have different foreflippers. Sea lions' flippers are wide and hairless. True seals have shorter foreflippers that are covered in fur. They also have long claws.

SEA CREATURE FEATURE

Sea lions can walk on land by turning their hind flippers forward. True seals hold their hind flippers straight out behind them. To get around, they slide on their bellies and roll from side to side.

Do you know which of these pinnipeds is a sea lion and which is a true seal? Look at their ears and their flippers for clues!

If you guessed the bottom image was of a sea lion, you're right! The top image is of a true seal.

HUNGRY HUNTERS

Sea lions eat all sorts of ocean animals, including crabs, fish, and even small sharks! In the Southern Hemisphere, they also eat penguins. Sea lions hunt alone or in small groups. They mostly hunt at night.

When searching for food, sea lions will dive as deep as 600 feet (183 m). Down that deep, it's cold and dark. Sea lions use their whiskers to sense fish in the dark water. They have thick **blubber** under their skin to keep them warm.

SEA CREATURE FEATURE

Sea lions don't need to drink water. They get the water they need from the fish they eat!

Sea lions are great at holding their breath. They can chase a fish underwater for several minutes before they need to come up for air.

COWS AND PUPS

Baby sea lions are called pups. Cows, or adult female sea lions, usually have one pup each year. Pups are born on land and can walk within half an hour. They soon have their first swimming and fishing lessons. Sea lion pups have much to learn, including how to stay away from sharks.

Sea lion pups stay together in rookeries while their mothers hunt. Rookeries are places where one of the cows watches over the pups while they sleep and play.

SEA CREATURE FEATURE

Sea lion rookeries are loud, but pups learn to recognize the sound of their mother's voice.

Sea lion pups are about 30 inches (76.2 cm) long when they're born, but they grow quickly. They stay with their mothers for up to three years.

SEA LION FAMILIES

Sea lions will often return to the same place each year to have babies. Several sea lions will gather in the same spot, and a **harem** will form. There are usually around 15 cows and their pups in a harem. There's also a single bull, or male sea lion. Several harems may live together.

Bulls bark very loudly when guarding their harems. They stay with their harems for about three months before returning to the ocean to look for new fishing areas. Cows and pups stay behind.

SEA CREATURE FEATURE

On land, a group of sea lions is called a colony. In the water, a group of sea lions is called a raft.

Groups of sea lions are often heard before they're seen. This is because they're always barking and roaring. They also like to climb over each other.

EASY TO TRAIN

If you've been to an aquarium or zoo, you may have seen a trained "seal" doing tricks. There's a good chance this talented animal was actually a California sea lion! California sea lions are friendly, playful, and smart. They're also easy to train.

California sea lions are the species most often used in circuses and other animal shows. They can use their front flippers for many tricks. They can shake hands, wave, and even pick up objects.

SEA CREATURE FEATURE

California sea lions can swim at speeds up to 25 miles (40.2 km) per hour. They're the fastest swimmers of all sea lion species.

This skilled sea lion is balancing a ball on its nose!

HELPING THE NAVY

The U.S. Navy has been training pinnipeds, including sea lions, since 1960. The Navy Marine Mammal Program (NMMP) trains sea lions to find and return objects that were dropped into the ocean. In many cases, **retrieving** these objects would be unsafe for people. Sea lions are great divers and can do the job quickly and safely.

NMMP sea lions sometimes wear special **harnesses** with underwater cameras attached to them. These cameras take pictures that can help keep our oceans safe during times of war.

SEA CREATURE FEATURE

The special NMMP harnesses are made so they don't get in the way while a sea lion is swimming.

NMMP trainers hope to use sea lions with camera harnesses to help find divers who get trapped underwater.

KEEPING SEA LIONS SAFE

People haven't always been kind to sea lions. We once hunted them for their skin, oil, and whiskers. Killing sea lions is now illegal in many places, but this doesn't always stop people hunting them. In some places, overfishing has left sea lions without enough to eat. Sea lions can also get caught in fishing nets.

Today, some sea lion species are **endangered**. However, people have been working hard to make the oceans safer for them. California sea lion populations have even been growing!

GLOSSARY

blubber: The fat on whales and other large marine mammals.

endangered: In danger of dying out.

flipper: A wide, flat "arm" used for swimming.

harem: A group of female sea lions with one male.

harness: A set of straps that goes around an animal's body, often used to control it.

hemisphere: One-half of Earth.

retrieve: To bring back.

snout: An animal's nose and mouth.

species: A group of plants or animals that are all the same kind.

webbed: Having skin between the toes, as ducks, frogs, and other animals that swim do.

whisker: A long hair growing near the mouth of some mammals, such as cats and otters.

INDEX

WEBSITES

Due to the changing nature of Internet links, PowerKids Press has developed an online list of websites related to the subject of this book. This site is updated regularly. Please use this link to access the list:
www.powerkidslinks.com/seac/slion